The Majesty of God
Meditative Poetry

Raymond S. Nelson

Stan Nelson, Artist

7301 Galoway
Wichita, KS 67212

Majesty of God

Cover photograph of Glacier National Park
by Raymond Nelson

Printed in the USA by Print Source Direct, Hillsboro, KS

ISBN 0-9713843-0-4

ILLUSTRATIONS

ACKNOWLEDGEMENTS

Family and friends have made incalculable contributions to this book. Margaret, my wife, is my best reader and respondent as well as word processor. My son John and daughter Fay have been vital sounding boards, and son Stan has devoted hours to creating the lovely line drawings. Son Tim was always an encourager. Julia Dagenais, fellow member of the Kansas Authors Club, gave helpful editorial hints. And my Quaker Sunday School class profitably discussed the poems as a classroom text.

(Titles of poems taken from earlier editions)
Carpe Diem from *At Home in Kansas*
The Cosmic Dance from *Prairie Sketches*
Doxology from *At Home in Kansas*
God of the Harvest from *Not By Bread Alone* and *At Home in Kansas*
God With Us from *Not By Bread Alone*
Great God of All from *Not By Bread Alone* and *At Home In Kansas*
Mystery from *Tracings* and *At Home in Kansas*
Orthodoxy, Heterodoxy from *Not by Bread Alone*, *Tracings*, and *At Home in Kansas*
Watching Faces from *Not by Bread Alone*
Wheels Within Wheels from *Not By Bread Alone*, *Tracings*, and *At Home in Kansas*.

TABLE OF CONTENTS

FOREWORD

"The heavens are telling the glory of God; and the firmament proclaims his handiwork. Day to day pours forth speech, and night to night declares knowledge. There is no speech, nor are there words; their voice is not heard; yet their voice goes out through all the earth, and their words to the end of the world." Psalm 19:1-4. RSV

"What can be known about God is plain to [humankind] because God has shown it to them. Ever since the creation of the world his invisible nature, namely, his eternal power and deity, has been clearly perceived in the things that have been made." Romans 1: 19, 20. RSV

I have written these poems in the spirit of these statements, avoiding the familiar phrases of dogma and doctrine that I have absorbed since childhood. The wonder of our world clearly posits a Creative Intelligence, a God who brought all things into being, who established natural laws, who sustains all things—yet remains invisible, inscrutable, and incomprehensible. It follows then that we humans walk by faith throughout life, trusting the guidelines established around the world by wise men and women over the centuries. It follows too that no one faith system is always and completely "right," but each one permits its participants to live happily and fruitfully.

Raymond S. Nelson

INTRODUCTION

In libraries there are many, many books, mountains of books, generations of words, attempting to explain that which cannot really be explained. Since before the time of writing, mankind strove to fathom the presence of life and the nature of God. Stories were told by the flickering light of the evening fire. Dreams were dreamed.

When marks in clay gained meaning, and leaves of papyrus were hammered into cohesive sheets that carried complex hieroglyphs, the words began to pile up. Some texts took on a life of their own, copied and re-copied until they found their way to us in a form that we have come to trust. Those words speak to us and we search within those familiar pages for an answer to life's questions. And yet, we have little that is irrefutable;

We have no absolute proofs. All is taken on large measures of faith. How are we to know of God?

There are those who search for proof—the doubting Thomases, who long to feel the palms of their savior. To know through experience, beyond any doubt, that all that has been told them is true. But there are no guarantees, no perfect evidence hidden amidst the many layers of words. We live with the survivors, the words which have been transmitted over centuries. When were they written, and by whom? Can we trust the witnesses?

Certainly, they are words we are comfortable with. These are the passages given to us in our youth. These are the words we have taken in with our mother's milk. Those who live in other places have grown up with different words, but they are no less true to them, no less comforting. Each knows that which comes with his own place, and the words fit.

Yet, greater than the words we live with, and the words we live by; greater than the religious structures established and perpetuated by man; is the certain text that God has given us. It is waiting there before us as it has always been. It is a text that has been eons of years in the making (merely a moment for a timeless God). There it is, a symphony of complexity and of life.

God's text is this world we live in, stretching out before us from sub-atomic particles to spiraling galaxies.

Look into a microscope at a droplet of pond water and you will see a microcosm filled with activity. All is urgency. Scale the Alpine peak or descend into the depths of the mid-Atlantic trench and you will find robust life. It is all around us. Watch a baby born in squalling perfection; turn to the swelling curves of the woman from which that child came, and marvel at her beauty; look at the mountain range that sits on the horizon, and think of how all this came to be. Every form—life's symmetry, its integration, its indomitable will—is truly a testament to a Majestic God. This text awaits a hungry reader—if only we may learn to read.

Stan Nelson

GOD

God is.
God is creator.
God is eternal now.
God is beyond good and evil.
God is mystery to finite human minds.

MYSTERY

The Maker donned a robe of light
Neatly lined with shades of night
To shield himself from human sight
And work his will in sovereign might.

God's garment hides his essence true
From human grasp and human view
Because "to know" means "to subdue."
And Mystery—once known—is through.

Daylilies

BEHIND THE VEIL

God is the circle squared
A sunbeam frozen fast;
God is voluble silence,
An atom punily vast.

God is bottomless height
A tower eternally low;
God is a jet black sun
Emitting a brilliant glow.

God is serene monsoons
Or blustery tranquil showers;
God is beyond our ken
As are my garden flowers.

ORTHODOXY

When dogma takes the place of faith
And creeds become enshrined,
Then cant enshackles thought itself
And chains bind every mind.

HETERODOXY

When people dare to dream and think
And leave some things unsure,
Then they can walk by faith
And trust the Spirit's overture.

("Today's heterodoxy is tomorrow's orthodoxy."
Father Josef Gregori)

PRAYER

I pray to God in silence
A hundred times a day.
I seldom get an answer
But I pray on anyway.

It may be superstition
And I tell God that it may
But I sense an inner power
So I just intend to pray.

I don't see many changes
In the things I pray about
Alteration has to start
With me, without a doubt.

I wake to God each morning,
I share my joys and pains,
I seek to walk as partner
With God who guides and reigns.

GREAT GOD OF ALL

Great God of all, accept our praise
As we our mortal voices raise;
We own your majesty and power
In this, our brief but joyful hour.

We strive to be our best for Thee
Despite our earthbound minds, we see
The bounties of Thy grace each day
Yet never fully grasp Thy way.

We are not yet what we shall be,
Thy shaping is not done. So we
Endure Thy patient hand which still
Transforms us all with wondrous skill.

Framed in weakness, formed of clay,
We join our voices now to say
We worship Thee, our help and stay,
Eternal God: past, future, and today.

Bison

DOXOLOGY

All nature is a hymn to God.
The liveliest brook, the lowest clod,
The placid pond, the hurricane
Join in a solemn choral strain
To match the music of the spheres,
A realm not tuned to human ears.

But hum of insect, song of birds
Blend into airs that can be heard,
That add to plaintive sounds of sheep
And cattle, moan of doves, the cheep
Of chicks, the howl of wolves, a round
Of notes which everywhere resounds.

All nature sings to those who hear,
To those, like Francis, who in sheer
Delight perceive the mighty voice
Of all creation raised in a choice
Motet, a harmony sublime,
Through all eternity and time.

GOD WITH US

The light exists in everyone
From birth to dying day
For God endowed each human soul
And lives in each always.

The light may flicker or burn low,
It may shine clear and bright,
Yet every person harbors God
Each moment day and night..

When things go wrong and lives collapse,
The light remains, though faint,
And shines within as truth and love
Restore without constraint.

The light of God sustains the mind
Of those who heed the way,
Bestowing inner peace and calm
As bolsters for each day.

MICRO-UNIVERSE

Every person is a universe,
A stunning harmony of head and heart,
Of mind and matter, blood and flesh and bone,
Where networks interlace to do their part,
Sustaining life in all their myriad ways—
Deriving vital energy from the tongue,
Repairing wounds, maintaining skeletal strength,
Circulating fluids, engendering young.

Consider too the power of memory,
Of complex ratiocinative skill,
Of passion, pride, and sensitivity,
Of powers, appetites, and focused will.
Imagination and creative pow'r
Add grace to all the elements
That make each one almost a mortal god,
Earth's prince, God's primal instrument..

ENIGMA

Men and women are a paradox,
Filled with hopes and dreams, but plagued by fears,
Benevolent and kind, but selfish too,
Purposeful and loving, till spite appears.

Endowed with reason many fail to think,
Gifted to create, instead destroy,
Provided with a will, but weak in spine,
Drift along, a bobbing errant toy…

Contradictions flourish, questions mount—
Lord of all creation? Or Nature's child?
Earth's mortal being? Or soul divine?
Endless fascination, truth beguiled.

STRIKING LIKENESS

If I am the image of God
Then God is the image of me.
Now that's not really odd...
Just look in a mirror and see.

The face in the glass is true
To the one looking on with wide eyes,
The image is faithfully you
And you study with no surprise.

The image of justice appears,
Compassion, intelligence, care,
Patience and love in their spheres
With knowledge and truth further pair.

But anger and jealous green eyes
Surface too, dark memories, hate,
Impatience, as plans go awry,
And frowns that harsh judgments create.

Creator and creature are like
The difference is one of degree,
For man is a being oblique
From God who remains mystery.

HERE? OR THERE?

God is nearer than a heartbeat
And farther than a star.
Anyone may find God
No matter where you are.

The spirit leads each one by faith
To God within or far
And asks no question how or why
No matter who you are.

SNAPSHOT

"Our God is a consuming fire,"
Yet "God is love" I read. In awe
I contemplate a being higher
Than I can imagine. Straw
Visions of divinity
Abound: a bearded Santa Claus,
A sentimental Amity,
Deus ex machina, of course…
A fearful judge of right and wrong,
Accountant for a Book of Life
Of human deeds both weak and strong,
And, then, an arbiter in strife…
A better view of God combines
The soft and hard, the kind and stern,
A Being far beyond the mind
Of man to fathom or discern.

Rimrock

VIDEO

God speaks to me from sunsets
And waving seas of grain,
I hear God's voice in rainbows
That curve above the rain.

I marvel at the mountains
That formed at God's command
And revel in the forests
That issued from God's hand.

God is surely present
In a world so rich and fair,
Creation bears God's hallmark
Apparent everywhere.

WHEELS WITHIN WHEELS

I contemplate the cycles
That govern daily life—
The ends and the beginnings
The peace that follows strife.

I watch a storm to silence
While braving wind and rain,
Then revel in the sunshine
That floods the earth again.

Each dawn gives way to evening
And life succumbs to death;
My son becomes a father
While I draw shorter breath.

The seeds of spring grow golden
And harvest grains roll in;
The summer's sun arcs lower,
Ere winter's snows begin.

I pause in meditation
On Mystery and Power
Revealed in constant motion
And worship in that hour.

GOD OF THE HARVEST

With apples picked and safely stored,
With wheat and corn and milo in,
We gather in Thy House, Oh Lord,
To offer thanks for everything.

We share Thy bounty at our board,
We lift our eyes to Nature's pride—
The season's harvest, Autumn's hoard—
And worship Thee—Thou dost provide.

We revel in each russet sash,
In maples crowned with crimson crest,
In reds and golds from frosty lash
Which warn of winter's coming rest.

We watch, we pray, we seek Thy face,
In all Thy matchless handiwork
We sense Thy care, we claim Thy grace,
We seek Thy signature to trace.

CARPE DIEM

All our yesterdays are filed away
In photos, mem'ries, and the scores of things
That fill our treasure chests. So, live today.
It's all we have. Commoners and kings
Stand equal at the threshold of each day.

Tomorrow is a phantom. It may or may
Not be. This moment is reality
And calls each soul to dream, then freely play
The game of life—each day can then well be
A playing field where winners wear the bays.

Scan the stars at night, the sun by day.
Touch a tree, some grass, or blossom. Taste
A plum, an apple, or a date. The way
To win is through such simple things not based
On fortune, rank, or what the hucksters say.

And living calls for loving too. Do stay
In touch with family, friends, a mate
Perhaps, and learn to love from early days.
The Wind of God blows through us to create
A caring fellowship. So, seize the day.

THE WORD

God speaks in many languages,
Many places, many times.
God's word is rife in rocks and trees,
In skies and seas, as Nature signs.

God speaks through human voices too,
The message from all lands, in days
Long past, today, and years to come
As the Spirit moves and truth conveys.

Sages spoke through Vedas, Eddas,
Tao Te Ching, Upanishads, Koran,
The Bible, Book of Mormon, that
Men might base their faiths thereon.

Faithful men and women live
Around the globe, serving God
In simple trust while calling out to
Allah, Elohim, or God.

Cottonwood

TREES I HAVE KNOWN

As we waited for our orange bus,
An ancient oak tree nurtured us
With its farflung arms, its stubby trunk,
Its twelve foot girth (a massive chunk),
A cooling shade from a whispering crown
Or shelter from rain pelting down.

A grove of beech an acre wide
With massive boles, soft light inside,
Smooth bark in gray, quiet, tall,
A sense of awe suffusing all...
It seemed a shrine inviting prayer
For those in silence gathered there.

A row of elm with stately mien,
Lordly stems and brilliant green,
Presided over shrubs and lawn
The family viewed each day from dawn
To dusk, till tragic loss one day...
Disease bore all six away!

Of many trees, our Bradford pear
Was special, graceful, sturdy, fair,
Blooming pearly white in spring,
Flaming red in fall, last fling,
Before she stripped and went to sleep
Ere winter's snows lay soft and deep.

SYMMETRY

Sunshine and rain,
Laughter and pain,
The two go together
In all kinds of weather.

Sunshine alone
Is a torrid zone.
Laughter unchecked
Gives a madhouse effect.

Rainfall alone
Causes floods we bemoan,
Pain without let
Is a burden beset.

Sunshine and rain,
Laughter and pain,
Balance each other
Like Father and Mother.

ORIGINALS

God leaves cloning to men—
No Dolly for him!
God deals with one-of-a-kind.
    Any person is a case in point—
    Unique fingerprint, footprint,
    Voice print, gene print.
No two trees or shrubs
Are exactly alike, and
Every snowflake is an original
Crystal tracery.
    The world is a stunning parade
    Of limitless one-of-a kinds.

FAUNA

"Tiger, Tiger, burning bright... Did he
Who made the lamb make thee?" And, may we ask,
Did God make ticks and lice and gnats and fleas?
And wolves and bears and lions? Whom shall we task

If not the God of all? The Master's hand
Has fashioned every whit. The gentle deer
And cow, together with the rest, were planned
And set against each other, never fear.

For why not jungle as well as Eden? Birth
Alone, without the counterpart of death,
Would trip the delicate balances of earth.
The wise creator gave all beings breath.

All living things subsist on living things,
So predator and prey fill roles each day
Fulfilling destinies, their hoops and rings
Set out from earliest times in full array.

WHIMSY

Most creatures reproduce in pairs.
It takes a male and female to produce
An heir—bacterium or ocelot!
But each has only half the gear for use

In reproduction. Surely God's caprice?
Consider all the dancing, strutting some
Go through to catch her eye, and all the wiles
And ploys she manages with arch aplomb.

MYTH

Men reach out to God through prayer,
Ritual, and poetry,
Creating meaning for themselves,
A cosmos to make sense of life.

Egypt worshiped Ra, the sun god,
Lauded Isis and Osiris,
Ulysses honored Jove and Juno
As they ruled from high Olympus,
Olaf prayed to one-eyed Odin,
Feared grim Thor but loved good Baldr,
Persians served Ahura-Mazda
Locked in strife with Ahriman.

The mysteries, the wonderment
Of sheer existence on the earth,
Become enshrouded in the myths
Recounted to explain the lot.

MASKS

They wear masks.
They all wear masks.
Their smiles and empty faces
Keep their secret selves so secure
That no one—
Wife or husband,
Child or parent—
Ever plumbs the depths
Of another's soul.

"Know yourself" said Socrates.
…such arrant nonsense!
If masks obscure the features
Of our fellows,
A soft and shifting miasma
Hides us from ourselves.
We are as inscrutable
And unknowable
As the One who made us.

The Chill of Winter

HOW LONG, O LORD?

When El Nino triggers storms and drouth,
Where are you, Lord?
When the Nile does not flood its banks,
Where are you, Lord?
When torrents fall, and rivers rage unchecked,
Where are you, Lord?
When monsoon rains fail, and lands lie parched,
Where are you, Lord?
When glaciers grow, and the earth is bitter cold,
Where are you, Lord?
When deserts spread, and sand dunes cover all,
Where are you , Lord?
When lightning strikes, and forest fires rage,
Where are you, Lord?
When earthquakes rock, and cities fall in ruin,
Where are you, Lord?
When the comet strikes the earth, and billions die,
Where will you be, Lord?

HOLY OF HOLIES

God is in his holy temple.
Let all the earth respond with awe,
Let mortal beings seek God out
To learn of God's eternal law.

Each man and woman is a fane
Where God abides, though oh so many
Do not sense the sacred flame
That burns within them constantly.

Sometimes the soul in silence hears
The still small voice from deep within
And learns to walk with God on paths
Of truth and love that make all kin.

You then can see it in their eyes.
The eye is window to the soul,
To the temple pure and clean,
Where God abides, and lives are whole.

A fane is a temple.

YOUR MOVE

We play the game of life with a player
Just and gracious, one who made the rules
And offers fair to help us make each move.
Mysterious, silent, generous, he vies
With us each day yet, like a father, gives
His child wide choices as he plays the field.
But if we cheat, miscalculate, or fail,
We find ourselves decisively ruled out.
Old Job played well, challenging his lot,
Just to learn that honesty and grit
Pay off. His friends, the well-bred Pharisees,
Were judged, found wanting.
Bernard Shaw played well,
Though scandalizing many as he voiced his views.
Schweitzer, Gandhi, Wallenberg, and King
Exemplify the best of players, saints
Among us, teaching us to play
The game with honor, courage, truth, and hope.

INSIGHT

The fresh green leaves of spring become in fall
 A dry brown carpet, sure the forests' pall
 As life gives way to death, and leaves return
To dust only to nurture life in turn.

The million seeds produced to make a tree…
Or fish… or child… while only one shall be,
Suggests not waste or prodigality
As much as certainty, or constancy.

In life and death, two faces for one soul,
The creature thrives in alternating roles,
Fulfilling God's eternal will and plan
Inscrutable and puzzling to man.

MEDITATION

Far from the sound of cataract,
Of tiger avalanche and crumbling cliff,
Of hurricane wind and monsoon moaning,
Of braying donkey and twittering finch,
Of thunderclap and erupting volcano,
Of trumpeting swan and crashing wave,
Of racing motor and blasting horn,
Of slamming door and booming bass,
    Comes the still small voice of God
    In the silence of one's own heart.

WATCHING FACES

Walk the streets and search the faces,
Sense the burdens, catch the graces
Flashed in fleeting smiles, grimaces,
From each passerby.

Placid surfaces on faces
Oft belie the desperate races
Run behind the dark fringed laces
On a pair of eyes.

Behind some still and passive faces
Cauldrons seethe in secret places—
Not the kinds of commonplaces
You'd expect to find.

Frozen smiles on frozen faces
Numb the terror at the bases
Of distracted minds, faint traces
Of the hidden scene.

Walk the streets and watch those faces,
Proper masks, like ancient vases,
Silent sounds from inner spaces—
Enigmatic planes.

EDELWEISS

Nature's scowls and smiles set the stage
For mankind's given roles from day to day.
Her laws are irresistible and firm;
She plays no favorites in life's ballet.

God made it so. The world's a perilous place
Where mankind early learned that love and care
Afford the only means to overcome the odds
And flourish as frail creatures share.

METAMORPHOSIS

In the beginning God created an infant
Universe which is still evolving.
Creation is not done. Heaven
And earth, galaxies and planets, continents
And oceans are forever thrusting outward…
Changing, growing, merging, spreading. Yearly
Elements of life emerge to dandle
On the knees of Mother Earth. Jungles
Introduce strange creatures to our scholars,
And hybridizers change old forms to new ones.
Dinosaurs and mammoths ranged our valleys
Countless years until convulsions altered
Modes of life and fresh new forms appeared.
Consider all the kinds of homo sapiens.
Genetic engineering alters offspring
So that changes in the future may occur
Faster than in the past. God's world emerges
Day by day according to God's purpose
An iridescent cosmic butterfly.

The Cycle of Life

THE GREAT CHAIN OF BEING

Earth teems with life
    From mites in honeybees
To eighty ton whales
    At the bottom of the seas.

Spores and pollens dance
    At all levels in the air
While moss and fungi probe
    The soil and tissues there.

Birds and parasites
    Abound in canopies
A league above the ground
    In old growth trees.

Lichens thrive on granite
    And termites on old logs
Releasing vital vapors
    As interstitial cogs.

Animals and men
    Fill their given places
Fulfilling destinies
    Like others in their races.

Did God imagine life?
    What creativity
And patient handiwork
    To set the stage we see!

IN THE BEGINNING

The newborn calf sucks its mother's teat;
The baby pig seeks a nipple, the one
She will always use; an infant child
Does not need instruction how to nurse...
All mammals know at birth just what to do.

The peeping chick, the quacking duckling, know
Just whom to seek for cover and for help.
The sightless kit and puppy mewl and yip
As parents lavish total care on them.
Even hawks and owls nurture young.

Such universal instinct cannot be
Pure chance, can it? Surely someone planned
For life to thrive in all its myriad forms
Far beyond mere flesh and skin and bone?
The stream of life affirms its source in God.

STORYBOOK

In the beginning God created earth
And heaven, a wondrous book to read
With loving care and thought. The opening page
Is lost in immemorial mists of time,
As comets, planets, asteroids, and stars,
With other elements, began their age-old
Cycles and their roles. Astronomers
Have read the story: Ptolemy, and Kepler,
Brahe, Copernicus, Hubble, Hale,
And more. The long-closed spheres burst open wide,
They say, and heavenly bodies raced in routes
Prescribed at dawn. Except for meteors,
Asteroids, and comets. These move
In isolated splendor through the skies,
Agents of destruction and creation
In their turn. Catastrophes occur
As astral bodies crash, no doubt the will
Of God, architect and maker of it all.
But out of evil goodness often comes.
When did trilobites and other modes
Of life appear. How? And when did reptiles
Rule the earth? Why must they die?
Did a comet's impact cause their fate?
From catastrophic moments rose
New life, mammalian life, besides the kinds
Persisting from the past. The earth is rich
As life-forms fill the land and sea
And air. We read with care to see
Beyond the order, power, beauty
Of the universe, to glimpse
The author of the wondrous tome.

GOD'S PALETTE

God first fashioned earth
By painting a swath of green for grass
And baby blue for sky.
God chose a frosty cream for dawn
And a rosy glow for dusk.
God's brush lay golden filaments on wheat,
Yellow on fresh hay,
Deep dark green on front range hills
With purple shadows far behind.
The pounding surf appeared in blues and grays,
Tipped with frothy white,
The shore a dusty, sandy tan,
Or black where water splashed on rocks and cliffs.
God dotted flowers in the fields,
Yellows, red, purple, orange, blue,
And dozens more,
Accenting browns and grays and greens.
God, like Wood or Bierstadt,
Must love color, judging from the finished canvas
We enjoy today.

COLOBAUGH POND

Tim sat in his borrowed rowboat,
Line in hand,
Almost hidden in the mist
Rising wispily from the placid pond.
I used to fish these waters,
Long ago,
Summer evenings,
Sometimes even through the winter's ice,
Catching mostly perch and bass.
I watched and listened,
Enchanted by the bullfrogs
Booming out in chorus far and near.
Water lilies, white among the dark green pads,
Spread out from the dock I sat on,
Disappearing slowly in the rising mist.
I wiped the beads of moisture from my can of Coke.
Water. I thought of God's prodigal hand.
Water. Two-thirds of the planet
Cased in water.
The murmuring brook on the flats.
The cool refreshing spring at home.
The deep artesian well.
The turgid, brackish pools in the swamp.
Streams, rivers, oceans, seas, lakes.
Water everywhere.

THE WIND

The wind has many faces. Gentle zephyrs
Smile on fertile fields and quiet towns,
But vicious cyclones rage across the land
Destroying limb and life with austere frowns.

Winds ride the ocean of air from highs
To lows, ruled by jet streams, heat and cold,
By valleys, ocean currents, hills, as God
Established Nature's laws in days of old.

Winds may bless and winds may damn. They melt
Great ice caps, whip up storms, propel wind mills,
Cause updrafts, wind shears, clear air turbulence,
As currents flow on mountains, plains, and hills.

Her names are legion: Santa Ana, foehn,
Chinook, simoom, sirocco, harmattan,
Khamsin, mistral, samiel, Rib Asfar
Ruwach, meltome... the list goes on.

Winds have turned the tide of history
Saint Joan at Orleans, the Spanish fleet
("God breathed and they were scattered," sang the English)
Two of many tales the bards repeat.

Winds surround the globe and impact life
At every level, ocean floor to highest peak,
Flowing softly, gently, loudly, wildly,
From the dawn of time till even as we speak.

Galaxy

SPIN SPAN SPUN

Whirling planets keep their axes as they spin,
Bulging as they do, while orbiting their stars.
The members of the Milky Way revolve within
The galaxy to form the cream of exemplars.

Electrons, protons swirl around their nuclei,
Building atoms, molecules, earth's building blocks.
Cyclones (hurricanes) turn around an eye
While roaring over oceans like a maddened ox.

Whirlpools like Charybdis form where currents grate,
Capsizing ships and terrorizing men at sea.
Magma circulating deep in earth creates
Magnetic lines that gird the earth tenaciously.

Spirals from the hand of God appear throughout
The universe from grandly sweeping nebula
To tiny maple seeds windmilling down to sprout
A hundred feet away—superb phenomena!

FIRE POWER

Fire, Fire, burning bright,
Flaming hearth by day or night,
Bubbling kettle, fragrant food,
Cozy warmth from blazing wood,
Glowing embers, source of light,
Centerpiece of each homesite.

Fire, Fire, burning bright,
Scorching earth by day and night,
Charring forests, searing plains,
Kindling fields for lack of rains,
Dwellings gutted, creatures killed,
Blackened ash when all is stilled.

Fire, Fire, burning bright,
Hearth or heath by day and night,
Gift of God for good or ill
(Uncontrolled or curbed by will),
Basic element we share—
But with constant care. Beware!

THE GAMUT

Mountain and molehill
Blue whale and bluefish
Mammoth and marten
Redwood and redbud
Peony and pansy
Mighty and minute
Each one in its place.

Hypnotic Stare

COVERT GLIMPSES

Nature is the garment of God—
Towering redwoods and sequoias,
Stately elms and robust oaks
Together with fragrant lilacs
And Rose of Sharon that share in the wonder
Of age-old life;

Lilies of the Valley and clear-eyed pansies
Line my gardens filled with roses
Peonies, daisies, Sweet William,
Vinca, azaleas, foxglove, and dahlias,
All symbols of the beauty of creation
And its maker;

Cats and dogs, cattle and swine,
Lions, hippos, zebras, panthers,
Otters, alligators, manatees and mice,
Range the seas and land, fulfilling
Purposes not fully clear to man
Yet faithful to the roles
Assigned to them;

The radiance of the sun
And shimmer of the moon,
The pulse of northern lights
Or wash of the Milky Way,
The sizzle of sharp lightning
And freshness of the following dawn—
All these are the glory of God.

EONS

God is in no hurry. Look around.
Discover fossil fish and birds that date
From mythic days, remains that have been found
In strata high and low from state to state.

And then consider reptile dinosaurs
With all their cousins, yes, with mammoths too.
Their eggs and bones and teeth and tusks and spoors
Invite a hundred theories with each clue.

Why have all these creatures lived? When
Exactly? How could fossil fuels be thrust
So deep within the earth? And then, again,
Why have forests turned to desert dust?

Why have other forests turned to stone?
How can that be? Trees that die today
Return to soil so that new growth alone
Is prime; no petrotrees are left this way.

Survey millenia then think how brief
Our memory is. We are ephemera.
The universe unwinds, and God's motif
Eludes the mind of man to sketch or draw.

FLUX

God's time is motion.
Stars and planets move and spin,
Coursing through the heavens,
Just as it has always been.

Consider then our sphere
With its double turn and sweep,
Bringing light and darkness,
Bidding us to wake or sleep.

God's time is process.
Seeds grow into beasts or trees
Which then mature and thrive
To ripe old age or cruel disease.

Continents divide,
And waves wear rock and strand,
Mountains crumble, rivers
Fill; there's change on every hand.

 Time is an illusion,
Mere measure of earth's pace,
For God eternal
Needs no sundial's face.

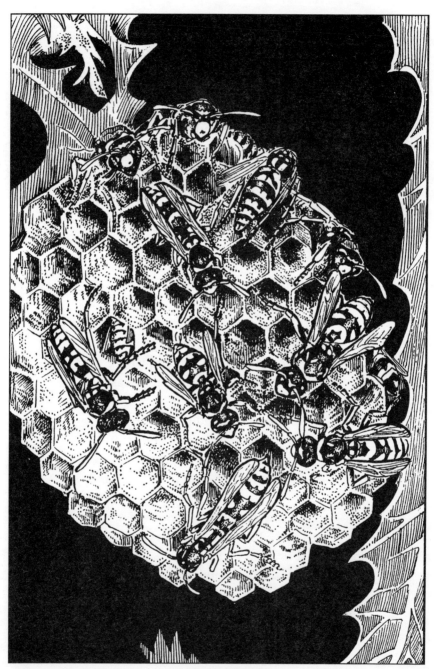

Ladies in Waiting

DESIGN

God's attention to detail
Knows no limit. Every creature
Is a marvel of design
Complete with every vital feature.

Camouflaged chameleons
And jagged jaguars blend
With light and leaves and stems and bark
In order to achieve their ends.

The iridescent butterfly,
More glorious than a Wyeth scene,
Dazzles human sight and flits
Across the fields in grace serene.

The lovely lilac blooms each year
Accompanied by daffodils
And tulips, crocuses, and flags
To form the vista Spring distils.

Did God decree that ants should free
Peony blossoms? Or that bees
Should pollinate the apple tree?
And that tulip bulbs must freeze?

The social ants and bees create
Communities where each performs
A varied role so that the whole
Assembly thrives as each conforms.

Every creature fills its place
On earth equipped with wondrous skill
To prosper till its dying day,
A hostage to the planner's will.

WHATEVER IS, IS RIGHT

Hale Bopp and Halley show up on time,
To the second.
The planet spins and sets the pendulum
At Greenwich.
Light speeds at a given
Rate, never wavering.
Energy is mass times the speed of light squared.
Water boils reliably and freezes predictably.
Semen and ovum, pollen and pistil work wonders.
DNA is an absolutely sound record of the race:
Order is the watchword of the universe,
Balance and harmony are the keys.

Convulsions of the sea or exploding mountaintops,
Rain forests turned to deserts,
Glaciers replaced by timbered valleys,
The North Pole inverted to the South,
Black plagues and famines run their courses,
Quanta sometimes behave randomly,
But these are all part of perfection.
Apollo and Dionysus are kin.
Every aberration is a stepping stone
To the future,
To an emerging, developing cosmos.
Out of chaos, order always comes.

COMING AND GOING

All life has its source in God.
The spark of life which vitalizes flesh
Comes from God "who is our home." The flame
Which burns unceasingly while breath shall last
Is lit when couples pair. The mystery
Of quickened flesh achieved when germ cells meet
Persists unsolved today. Egregious men
Attend the flesh with marvelous results,
But of the spirit, life itself, they have
Not much to say. Sages through the ages
Simply shrugged and said, "God is the source of all.
When breathing stops, the soul returns to God
Who wrought the miracle of living flesh."
The good, the bad, the fair, the foul will one day
Join the Source of Life itself.

PSALMODY

When Thor was at his anvil
And lightning lit the sky
All nature waited breathless
Then made a swift reply.

The wind blew through the treetops
The leaves and branches sighed,
The windchimes in the arbor
Sounded far and wide.

The dogs spoke out in chorus
Or answered one by one,
The roosters added comment
Not to be outdone.

The jays and finches chattered,
The wrens and redbirds sang,
The crows and feisty sparrows
Added voice till heaven rang.

The cattle on the hillsides
Lowed or bellowed loud
While sheep and lambs called softly
To each other in that crowd.

The coyotes on the prairie
Sounded out to all
While wolves in lonely places
Added plaintive calls.

The crickets in the meadow
And hoppers in the field
Syncopated rhythms
From platforms well concealed.

The buzzing flies persisted,
Mosquitoes dipped and droned,
The honeybees hummed softly
As their fellow hornets moaned.

The ocean waves lapped gently
On rugged cliffs and rocks,
The stones themselves vibrated
As true as Huygens' clocks.

Such sounds of earth blend daily
As humble voices raise
To God the great creator
Their joyful songs of praise.

The Overlook

EARTH'S HALO

A marvel of God's miracles is light—
The wonder of the world revealed through sight—
As sun and moon and stars subdue the night!
Each breaking dawn is heaven's gift outright.

Prisms in the raindrops fill the sky
With color as a rainbow arches high,
And storm-born lightning-flashes beautify
The vault above and captivate the eye.

Whether sunbeams or resplendent rays
Of lightning fill the sky, either way
The miracle of light sustains the play
Of life in all its forms from day to day.

ONENESS

All life proceeds to death, and death sustains
All life, but then all life regenerates
In young, an endless cycle God ordains
To keep the wondrous masterplan intact.

Trees and plants communicate, they say,
And trees and animals reciprocate
In what they breathe; the daily interplay
Of living things leads many, then, to state:

"All life is one. The tree of life has root
In nature's earliest day, since when bole
And branch and twig have swelled till they have put
The present growth in place, a vibrant whole."

SEEDS AND WEEDS

A gardener, like God, deals with life
And death each day. He sows the seeds that sprout
To corn or beans, or lily, fern or rose,
Then turns with hoe to ferret out a weed
Invading a forbidden bed.
All plants are useful, worthy scions,
Whether understood and prized or not.
The gardener decides. He proffers love
And care on one but not the other. Yet
Every one is precious in its place,
Whether mulch or hoe become his choice.

PAIRS

All things come in pairs. The number two
Is at the heart of all. We do but choose
From best or worst, the good or bad, each day
To create the essence of our way.

Angels and gargoyles on cathedral roofs
Speak in stone of that ancient truth, proofs
Of the medieval hint that evil and good
Entwine themselves, even as they would.

The rain and sun make up another pair,
Just as life and death in their affair
Combine to be extensions of man's soul.
A proper balance guarantees a whole.

The Chinese long ago divided yin
From yang, the male from female. They had been
Perceiving polar tensions long before
The West began to borrow ancient lore.

Antimatter must exist, a pole
For common matter; why not a deep black hole
As well to pair with stars and moons
If all things harmonize and hum in tune?

Winter and summer, parka and swimsuit, reach
Across the zodiac, year after year, each
As far apart as war and peace, twin states
As tense as lamb and tiger and their fates.

What then of up and down, or in and out?
And, I might add, of whisper and of shout?
Or sleep and wake? Or fat and thin? Of long
And short, of soft and hard, of right and wrong?

See the computer buff who mixes ones
And zeroes to make a tool that helps reach suns
And moons galore. Just think! Two digits let
It all take place, a tool as good as it gets.

READY OR NOT

God played hide and seek one day
And tucked the wealth of worlds away,
Pure zinc and iron, oil and gold,
Copper, silver, lead and coal.
Ever since men play the game
And, having found a lode, lay claim.

West of Eden

WORK IN PROGRESS

As Rembrandt sketched with colors dark and light
To fashion masterpieces on broad planes,
God works his canvases with sun and shade
To fashion views that dazzle human sight.
The Artist uses blacks and brilliant strains
To highlight prairie scenes and mountain glade.

A world awash in floods and hurricanes,
A world with cyclones, lightning bolts and hail,
With earthquakes, deserts, forest fires and ice
Contrasts Arcadian meadows, ripening grains,
Stately copses, mountain streams, a vale
Where lilies bloom, an island paradise.

The world attests creative artistry
On every hand. Nature's laws, though grim
At times, are still the Master's perfect plan,
As dazzling darkness blends with light to be
The means to chiaroscuro—surely a hymn
To Mystery since the world began.

STEP BY STEP

God set the worlds in motion
And established Nature's laws
That guide th' unfolding cosmos
And link effect with cause.

The creature poses questions
And speculates at will,
But clear and simple answers
Evade all mortals still.

"To know" is clearly futile
Beyond the here and now,
Yet the sphere of spirit
Is as sure as seers avow.

I solve the matter simply.
I walk by faith each day,
With faith in God the maker,
My fragile life's mainstay.

THROUGH A GLASS DARKLY

No one knows the mind of God
Though presumptuous voices prate,
It's just as though her kitten knew
The deepest thoughts of Mistress Kate.

Why were mastodons destroyed?
And why does climate change?
Why the glaciers? Why fierce storms?
And what makes weather patterns strange?

Why do the innocent suffer? And why
Do some die young? Why does age
Decay? And what is this thing called luck?
Why is there lust and hate and rage?

We have no answers to such questions.
Sacred writ is mute. We only see
The underside of God's design
Where shadows dim the broidery.

NATURE

This ordered world, the universe,
Proceeds under natural law,
For God is separate from all handiwork.
Cyclones, floods, convulsive quakes
Are as natural
As gentle rain and balmy summer days,
As men and animals,
As flowers, grass, and trees.
God made it so.
God's creative hand, and artist's eye,
Are everywhere apparent
In the blend of shadows and sunshine,
Of blacks and grays and whites,
Yet God remains apart.

SEEING IS BELIEVING?

Lines of force surround us,
Invisible but real,
They penetrate our being
But we neither see nor feel.

There's gravity and gamma,
Xray and infrared,
Magnetic fields and cosmic rays
And ultraviolet.

An unseen world surrounds us,
Invisible but real,
Eternal in God's wisdom
Though we neither see nor feel.

TERRA FIRMA

I grew up with stones and trees and soil
Almost unable to dig a hole for seed
Because of rocks and roots. My daily toil
Involved an axe to cut the wood we'd need
To fill the grate and stoke the kitchen stove.
Stone fences edged our land, marking lines
From long ago when men and boys strove
To clear the land for gardens and some swine.

But through neglect the little fields returned
To wilderness, and Dad set out to clear
Our land once more. In doing so I learned
That things of earth are as firm as they appear.
We blasted rock and cleared the land of trees,
We battled roots and stumps and stones and shale
While building roads and making acres free
From rubble, sticks, and brush through our travail.

In retrospect, I think of Plato's theme
That earth is mere illusion; that at bed
All things are energy and only seem
To be. But when I roundly bumped my head
Those days, I knew the limb was hard. And real.
"Which is it, then?" you ask. Well, both are true.
Electrons fill their places, while I feel
The solid earth within my grasp and view.

Tidal Wave

ATLANTIS, ET AL.

The rocks and hills and plains cry out
In muted universal shout
Of cataclysm on the earth.
They tell of floods that ranged the girth
Of Terrasphere, of tidal waves
That reached to highest mountain caves,
Of trees and rocks and cities lost
And driven deep or tempest tossed.
All life was threatened, mostly lost
(Some bodies kept in mire or frost),
All cultures ravaged, little left,
The few survivors sore bereft.
They speak of mountains burning bright
As lava flamed, a frightful sight,
As if the globe itself were dead
And passing on in lurid red.
They tell of hail from outer space
Of meteors which rained in place,
Of comets wandering close to earth
To tilt earth's axis, poles reversed,
A sun held still to lengthen day
Till darkness fell and long held sway.
When light appeared, the earth was changed
As plains emerged where hills once ranged
And mountains soared from ocean floors
While deserts spread from dry lake shores.
The evershifting earth seems sound
But what has been may well rebound
And bring to naught all we hold dear:
Our lives, our earth, our cosmophere.
The voices from the past are clear
Though mankind sifts and probes the austere
Word: what is God's will and plan?
And where, if anywhere, is man?

RAGNAROK

What has been will be.
An earth in agony
Will once again convulse
With spasm-like impulse.

Earth's long established calm
Will dissipate like dawn
When God permits the Norns
To blow their fateful horns.

The dreadful day will come
(The planet will succumb)
To terminate the age
And scour history's page.

The end of time is sure
Though God's intent obscure.
The hour is far from clear—
It may be far… or near.

Ragnarok is Old Norse for "doomsday,"
and the Norns are Fates.

MT. FUJI

The hoary mountain fastness touched the sky
As I idly ran a speculative eye
On ridges, trees and crags and cliffs and snow
(A heady panorama from below)
And thought how people long have looked to hills
As the dwelling place of gods, where goods and ills
Are judged—offerings and sacrifice
Advanced according to a priestly price…
Olympus, Fuji, Sinai, Horeb, names
Familiar to us all through faith's stern aims.
The solid mass evoked a sense of awe
As I pondered the Creator and the laws
Of Nature long set down: volcanic bed
So earthquake prone; glacier ice widespread
Across the vales; erosion rubble left
In piles; tidal flotsam bound in cleft
And stratum; alpine meadows rich in bloom.
I pondered these and knew I might presume
The seeming-solid mountain is as frail
And fragile as a dainty wedding veil.
Well, not quite. Suffice to say that things
Of earth are transient. Neither serfs nor kings
Can change our enigmatic human lot.
Nothing can escape God's sweeping fiat:
Let chance, decay, and alteration be,
Lest creation be a static entity.

GREAT PLAINS

The horizon marks the seam
Produced by earth and sky
When sutured by my eye
On the broad Midwestern plain.

The mile roads mark huge squares
For pasture, wheat, and hay,
While creeks and railroads stray
At angles anywhere.

The air is crisp and clean
So soil and field and grain
And tree, in sun and rain,
Create a pristine scene.

The crystal canopy
That arches day and night
Above this space invites
The viewer pause… and see.

Fossilized Crustacean

THE COSMIC DANCE

Icecaps melt and icecaps grow;
Earthquakes rend the face of earth;
Volcanic lava burns all things;
Cyclonic winds lash out to strow
The earth with trash. But soon rebirth
Occurs: from rubble order springs.
                Nothing stays the same.

Ancient forests long since stone;
Seaborn fossils found on high;
Mammoth bones on rolling plains;
Forgotten towns long overgrown
And fabled empires lost to eye
Speak loud of shifts no one explains.
                Nothing stays the same.

Nations live and nations die;
Systems work and systems fail
In faith and polity and war;
Armies fight and armies fly,
Statesmen seek a stable vale
While borders change and ruffians roar.
                Nothing stays the same.

Midwestern plains were once a sea,
Then glaciers ground across the land.
Dinosaurs and mammoths ranged
Where later buffalo roamed free,
We cannot stay Dame Nature's hand;
We can at best concede what's changed.
                Nothing stays the same.

Stars are born each day, and die;
Oak trees topple, acorns sprout;
Raging rivers gouge their banks;
Scorching winds make sand to fly
In brand new deserts caused by drought—
All rounds of Nature's endless dance.
                Nothing stays the same.

THE GRANDEUR OF GOD

If creation is so grand
What must the creator be?
The stellar sweep above
Speaks of majesty

While the glory of the earth
Attests an artist's hand
Unmatched in pow'r and grace
Expressed in sea and land.

The viewer stands in awe
Of a world so wondrous fair—
Its mountains, plains, rivers,
Trees, and oceans rare—

He lauds the Ancient One,
Resplendent in all things,
The source of heav'n and earth,
And lets God's praises ring.

SENTINEL

When dark descends
Or rain portends.
   The tulip closes up;
When dawn ascends
And light attends
   The petals form a cup.

MANDALA

The Master caught an ion
Pushed electrons toward a pole,
Reached for handy protons,
Spun the whole
Into an ordered mass.

The unseen became the seen,
The immaterial thus was matter,
A wedding of two spheres
That since has been
A thriving partnership.

The two live on together,
Millenia racing by,
Creation persevering
While patient sages try
To understand.

But nothing is forever.
Life and death are one,
Mandated by the Master;
When the union is undone
The cosmos will uncoil..

The Indian term Mandala is a
schematized representation of the universe

SEESAW

We live halfway between our memories
    And our dreams,
Half involved with solid facts
    And half with seems.

The past is grist for recollection,
    The future hope,
While all that's been is history,
    Seek now a horoscope.

Remembering is a blessing
    Or a curse;
Tomorrows will unfold
    Chapter and verse.

THE SOURCE

Ah, the mystery of life,
Called by some elan vital,
By others the Life Force,
Driving onward, upward,
Far beyond the green fuse
That drives flower, tree,
The sprouts of grass that
Lead life forward,
Teasing men and women
Almost out of thought.

One sage put it Reverence
For Life, seeing God
In everything that lives
And built a faith thereon.

Every living thing is holy,
Says the poet, silent voice
Of the inscrutable, ineffable
Source of all creation.